THE EARTH'S RESOURCES

Richard and Louise Spilsbury

Evans

TITLES IN THE SCIENCE IN FOCUS SERIES:
DIGITAL TECHNOLOGY   THE EARTH'S RESOURCES   GENETICS
THE HUMAN BODY   THE SOLAR SYSTEM   WEATHER

Produced for Evans Brothers Limited by
Monkey Puzzle Media Limited
Gissing's Farm, Fressingfield
Suffolk IP21 5SH, UK

Published by Evans Brothers Limited
2A Portman Mansions
Chiltern Street
London W1U 6NR

VISIT OUR WEBSITE
Evans
www.evansbooks.co.uk

First published 2006
© copyright Evans Brothers 2006

The right of Richard and Louise Spilsbury to be identified as the authors of this Work has
been asserted by them in accordance with the Copyright, Designs and Patents Act 1988.

British Library Cataloguing in Publication Data
Spilsbury, Richard, 1963
The Earth's Resources – (Science in focus)
1.Natural Resources – Juvenile literature
I.Title II. Spilsbury, Louise
333.7

ISBN 0 237 53095 3
13-digit ISBN (from 1 January 2007) 978 0 237 53095 2

Editor: Clare Weaver
Designer: Jane Hawkins
Picture researcher: Shelley Noronha
Artwork by Michael Posen

Picture acknowledgements:
Ecoscene 18 (Quentin Bates), 19 bottom (Chinch Gryniewicz); Getty Images 3, 8 (Grant Faint/The
Image Bank), 9, 23 (Daniel Smith), 24 (Colin Molyneux/The Image Bank), 28 right (Pascal Le
Segretain), 33 top; MPM Images front cover top left (Corbis Digital Stock), front cover centre left
(Creative Collection), 25 top (Corbis Digital Stock), 39; Panos Pictures 13 bottom (Piotr Malecki), 27
top (Chris Stowers), 36 (Ariane Van Buren); Science Photo Library 29 (Volker Steger), 31 (Martin
Bond); Still Pictures front cover main image (Jorgen Schytte), 6 (Mark Edwards), 7 (Mark Edwards),
10 (SJ Krasemann), 11 (Ron Giling), 12 (Masino), 13 top (Mark Edwards), 15 top (Chlaus Lotscher),
16 (Russell Gordon), 17 (Domingo Rodrigues/UNEP), 20 (Leuchtges/UNEP), 21 (Helmut Clever/UNEP),
22 (Klaus Rose), 25 bottom (Otto Stadler), 27 bottom (Roger De La Harpe), 28 left (J&L Weber), 32
(Mark Edwards), 35 (Jorgen Schytte), 37 (Alice Garik), 38 (Zhao Weiming/UNEP), 41 (Theresa de
Salis); Topfoto.co.uk 15 bottom, 19 top, 30 (R Frazier/The Image Works), 34 (Michael Thompson/
The Image Works).

CONTENTS

WHAT ARE RESOURCES?

Resources are things the Earth provides that people need and use, such as energy, water and raw materials for making things. As people carry on their normal lives, they use up resources.

◄ Water is only a useful resource for these children if it is clean enough to drink or wash in. Polluted water is not safe to use.

DIFFERENT KINDS OF RESOURCES

Some resources, such as the air we breathe, the water we drink and the food we eat, are vital for life. We could not survive without them. We could live without many other kinds of resources, but not without a drastic change in lifestyle. For example, we rely on energy from resources, such as fossil fuels, to cook food, keep us warm or cool, power vehicles and machines, and run our information systems.

Mineral resources, such as those we use to make metals, are also central to our everyday lives. Without metal, what would surgical instruments, trains and coins be made of? Other kinds of resources are important because they enhance life, such as wood for musical instruments or gemstones for jewellery.

RENEWABLE AND NON-RENEWABLE

Resources can also be divided into two general types. Renewable resources are those that will not run out, such as sunlight, which is continually being renewed, however much we use.

Non-renewable resources are those that will one day run out, such as fossil fuels. They are non-renewable because it would take millions of years to replace the quantity we are using.

▲ Trees are a renewable resource if we allow time and space to grow new trees to replace those we cut down.

POPULATION AND RESOURCES

The global (worldwide) population is expected to grow from 6 billion to over 8 billion by the year 2030. There are many reasons for this, including better, more widespread healthcare and improved sanitation. In future, a rising population will use up more and more of the planet's resources.

But resource use is not evenly spread over the globe. For example, richer people are using up some resources, such as oil, more quickly than poor people are. This is because they can afford to buy oil-guzzling cars, or new plastic gadgets, from toys to laptops, which are made partly from oil. The more resources people use, the greater the effect is on our shared environment, from air pollution to habitat destruction.

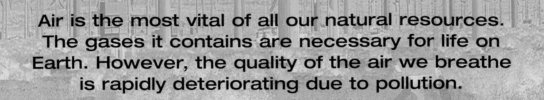

AIR

Air is the most vital of all our natural resources. The gases it contains are necessary for life on Earth. However, the quality of the air we breathe is rapidly deteriorating due to pollution.

AIR CONTENTS

Air is a mixture of gases in the atmosphere surrounding the Earth. Over three-quarters of air is nitrogen and the rest is nearly all oxygen. About 1 per cent of air is argon, carbon dioxide and trace gases. Trace gases are gases that occur in very small quantities in the Earth's atmosphere. There are also varying amounts of water vapour carried by air. This is visible in clouds, fog or mist, when it condenses. Floating around in air are many tiny particles, including dust, pollen and bacteria.

OXYGEN

Almost every organism on Earth needs oxygen for respiration. Without it, they would die.

▲ Clean air is a key ingredient for the survival of almost all living things. Aquatic animals, such as fish, can get the oxygen they need from water, but marine mammals, such as this orca, have to surface to breathe it in.

Respiration is not the same as breathing. It is a chemical reaction between oxygen and sugars from food that happens in cells. The reaction releases energy that is used for growth, making new body parts and moving. It also releases a waste product, carbon dioxide. Many animals, including people, breathe in air to get the oxygen they need for respiration. Plants take in oxygen through tiny holes in their leaves and roots.

THE ATMOSPHERE

The atmosphere maintains the temperature on Earth at the right level for life to exist. Heat from the Sun hits Earth, but not all bounces back into space. This is because greenhouse gases in the atmosphere trap heat, rather like a duvet. Greenhouse gases include carbon dioxide and methane. A layer of ozone (a special type of oxygen) in the atmosphere, about 40 kilometres above us, shields the Earth from harmful UV (ultraviolet) radiation from the Sun. Winds in the atmosphere transport clouds of water vapour around the globe, creating rain and the other types of precipitation, such as hail and snow, which living things rely on.

CHANGING ATMOSPHERE

Smoke from power stations, industries and vehicles is gradually polluting the Earth's atmosphere. Most vehicle engines burn fuels that release poisonous waste exhaust gases into the atmosphere. Tiny polluting particles in these gases can cause heart and lung disease. In parts of California, USA, over 100 out of every 100,000 people die from illnesses caused by breathing in these particles.

Waste gases from vehicles, and gases such as carbon dioxide released from factories and power stations, join other greenhouse gases in the air. When greenhouse gases increase, they trap more and more heat in the atmosphere. Many scientists believe this process, called global warming, is already affecting our climate and melting polar ice caps and glaciers around the world.

▼ There are already over 600 million privately owned cars in the world – that's one for every ten people.

FRESH WATER

Water covers three-quarters of our planet, but most of it is sea water. Less than 1 per cent of all the water on Earth is fresh water that we can use.

DOMESTIC USE

Fresh water is a vital resource for life – you can go weeks without food, but only days without drinking water. But we use water for many other things, besides drinking. In homes, people use water for cooking, washing, cleaning and sanitation. It is also used for leisure, for example, in swimming pools. Much of the water used in homes is piped from rivers, lakes and reservoirs, or from underground water sources.

The problem is that fresh water is not evenly distributed across the planet. Millions of people around the world do not have access to clean, safe water. This is because they might live in a highly populated dry country, or because water is too expensive to buy, or because the only water available is polluted or unfit to drink. The United Nations suggests that each person needs at least 50 litres of water a day for drinking, washing, cooking and sanitation. But in many parts of the world, such as Africa, people have to walk several hours a day to collect just a few litres.

INDUSTRIAL USE

Almost every industry you can think of – whether it produces metals, wood, paper, chemicals, shoes, or other products – uses water in some part of its production process. Industries use water as a raw material, a solvent, a coolant, to transport goods and, in the case of hydroelectric power, as an energy source. For example, it takes 148,000 litres of water to make one new car and its tyres. And, on average, agriculture uses up to 70 per cent of all fresh water across the world. Most of this is taken for irrigation (watering crops).

◀ Farming is a water-hungry industry. These enormous sprinklers are irrigating rows of cabbages.

▲ This polluted water is flowing out of a cotton-bleaching factory. It has the potential to damage nearby fresh water supplies.

PEOPLE AND POLLUTION

The total amount of natural fresh water available to us never changes. It simply circulates between the oceans, land and sky in the processes of evaporation and condensation in the water cycle. The problems we face are that people are reducing the amount of fresh water available by taking too much, too quickly, from some sources, and are polluting others.

Fresh water pollution comes from waste, sewage, industry, and pesticides and fertilisers that run off fields into water supplies. It is expensive to clean and purify polluted water and many countries do not have systems in place to do this. In developing countries, 70 per cent of industrial waste is dumped untreated into water, and around 12 million people a year die from diseases that are caused by dirty water and inadequate sanitation.

EVIDENCE FOCUS

HOW MUCH WATER?
Use the following data to work out roughly how much water you use each day. Is it as much as the average US citizen, who uses up to 380 litres a day?

Washing hands	0.95 litres
Brushing teeth	3.8 litres
Flushing toilet	19 litres
Laundry (per load)	114 litres
Showering	114 litres
Taking a bath	151 litres
Washing car	76 litres
Washing dishes (by hand, with water running)	38 litres
Washing dishes (by machine)	57 litres
Watering lawn (30 minutes)	908 litres

Include 2 litres of water taken in through food and drink each day.

Now, try to find out ways of conserving water. For example, turning off the tap while you brush your teeth saves 15 litres a minute!

SOIL

It might be 'dirt' to some people, but the layer of soil covering much of the Earth's land is one of our most important natural resources. Farmers need healthy, fertile soil to grow plentiful crops, and people rely on food crops for life.

WHAT IS SOIL?

There are many different kinds and types of soils, but basically soil is a combination of tiny particles of rock, water, air and humus. Rock particles come from rock that is slowly broken down by weathering – the action of wind, rain, sunshine and ice – over millions of years. Humus is decayed plant and animal matter, formed from dead organisms or the waste they produce when alive. A fertile patch of soil takes millions of years to form.

LIFE IN THE TOPSOIL

Layers of soil on the land vary in depth, but topsoil is the fertile layer of earth nearest the surface. Topsoil has the right amounts of humus, minerals, water and oxygen for seeds to germinate and plant roots to grow. Organisms that live in the topsoil break down the organic waste in humus. As they do so, they release into the soil nutrients that make it fertile. The particles of rock release minerals into the soil, which plants also need to grow healthily.

▲ Around one third of all land across the world is used for farming.

FACT FOCUS

SOIL COMMUNITY

One square metre of fertile soil can contain over 1,000 million organisms. This astonishing community includes small invertebrates – worms, millipedes, flatworms – and insects, such as springtails. As the invertebrates eat waste, they break it down into tiny pieces. Other members of the soil community, the bacteria and fungi, decompose these pieces into nutrients. Soil animals also tunnel through soil, mixing in the nutrients and creating gaps where air and water can gather.

▲ When land is cleared of plants, strong winds can blow as much as 150 tonnes of topsoil off each hectare every hour. This dust storm in Ethiopia is disappearing topsoil.

▶ As the population increases, farmers need to grow more food, but also conserve soil resources.

SOIL DEGRADATION

When topsoil is damaged or lost, this greatly reduces the amount of farmland available for growing plants. By 2005, about 15 per cent of once-useful land had been degraded by human activities. In Australia, almost one third of fertile farmland has been lost. The process by which soil, that was once thick and fertile, becomes thin and low in nutrients is known as desertification.

Desertification happens when topsoil becomes so dry and dusty that it is blown away or washed away. This can happen because of intensive farming methods, for example when too many livestock graze an area constantly, or

when there is overuse of harsh chemical fertilisers. It can also happen when people pump too much water from below ground for irrigation, so that the soil above dries up, or when irrigation water brings salts from below ground to the surface. The salts dry out and harden the soil, making it unsuitable for growing plants.

Some farmers use farming methods that help to conserve the soil. Instead of attacking micro-organisms with pesticides, they encourage insects that eat pest species. Rather than using artificial fertilisers, farmers rotate crops, use animal manure, and plant environmentally friendly manure crops that enrich the soil.

PLANTS

Plant resources are the source of food for almost every living thing on Earth. As well as food, we rely on plant resources for many other things, such as medicines.

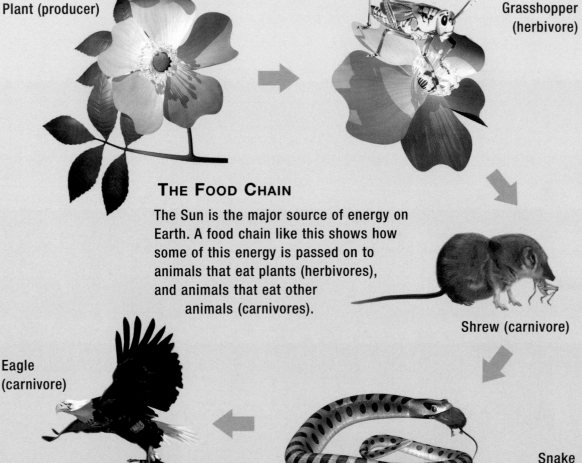

Plant (producer)

Grasshopper (herbivore)

THE FOOD CHAIN

The Sun is the major source of energy on Earth. A food chain like this shows how some of this energy is passed on to animals that eat plants (herbivores), and animals that eat other animals (carnivores).

Shrew (carnivore)

Eagle (carnivore)

Snake (carnivore)

PLANTS FOR FOOD

Plants are producers. They use the energy in sunlight to produce food, in a process called photosynthesis. Plants trap light energy using a pigment in their leaves called chlorophyll. Using water sucked in through their roots, and carbon dioxide from the air, which they take in through their leaves, plants make their own food – glucose (sugar).

When animals eat plants, or eat other animals that have eaten plants, they use this energy from the plant glucose to live and grow. This means that plants are the first link in almost

▶ When we eat beef or drink milk from a cow we benefit from the grass plant's ability to trap sunlight energy.

every food chain on Earth. Plants trap only around 1 per cent of all the solar energy that reaches the planet, but that is enough to provide energy to give life to almost every organism on the globe!

OTHER USES OF PLANTS

As well as plant foods such as cereals, fruit, vegetables, nuts and seeds, plant resources are also used to make drinks. Coffee is made with dried seeds from the coffee plant, tea from leaves of a variety of camellia bush and juice can be made from fruits and vegetables.

Some plant parts are used to make spices, such as the stem of the ginger plant and dried chilli fruits. Many medicines are made from plant extracts. For example, digitalis, which is used to treat some patients with heart problems, comes from the leaves of the foxglove plant. Essential oils are extracted from plant parts to make cosmetics and perfumes, or to add scent to bath oils and shampoos.

FEEDING THE WORLD

Across the world today, around 800 million people do not have enough to eat to be healthy. In part, this may be because they live in places without fertile soil, or a suitable climate for growing many crops, but the main reason is poverty. In rich, developed areas, such as Europe and North America, more food is being produced than people need. In poorer regions of the world, such as parts of Asia and Africa, most farmers do not have enough money to build the irrigation systems they need, or to buy the tools and seeds they require to grow enough to feed their own families, let alone supply others.

◀ At one time, all cloth dyeing was done using plant parts such as leaves, bark and flowers. Today, concern that some synthetic dyes are harmful means there is new interest in natural dyes.

HISTORY FOCUS

NORMAN BORLAUG (1914–1977)
In the 1960s, American scientist Norman Borlaug bred a new type of wheat plant that resisted disease and produced lots of grain. This sparked the 'green revolution' when new, high-yield varieties were grown in poor countries such as India and Pakistan. Borlaug won the Nobel Peace Prize in 1970 for his contribution to feeding the world's growing population.

WOOD

Wood is the hard, inner part of tree trunks, branches and stems. Wood is a renewable resource that we can use to make many different things.

TIMBER

Timber means useful wood. It often comes from tree trunks. The wood inside a tree trunk is dead. As it dries up, it becomes very hard and tough. Its high strength-to-weight ratio makes timber ideal for many building products, including window frames, walls, scaffolding, sheds, boats and furniture. Wood can also be cut and carved into many shapes: when polished its grain can look very attractive.

Timber is usually divided into softwoods and hardwoods. Softwoods come from coniferous trees, such as pine and fir. Hardwoods come from slower-growing, broad-leaved trees, such as oak and teak.

CELLULOSE AND PULP

Many paper products, including card, packaging, magazines and newspapers, are made from wood pulp. Most pulp is made from wood from softwood trees. Steam and chemicals break down wood chips to separate them into cellulose fibres and other wood components. The other wood components are removed to leave the cellulose. Cellulose is tough and fibrous, and forms part of the cell walls in plant cells. The cellulose fibres

◄ Once tree trunks and large branches have been cut down, the bark is removed and they are sliced into pieces to make timber.

are mixed with water and chemicals to make wood pulp. This pulp is then drained, squashed, rolled and dried to form sheets of paper.

FORESTS UNDER THREAT

Over 11 million hectares of forest are lost throughout the world each year. Most are cleared to make space for buildings or farming, or cut down for timber or pulp. Damaging forest ecosystems threatens vast numbers of plant and animal species, which are robbed of their habitats. Deforestation (the clearing of forests) also damages the balance of gases in the atmosphere, which we rely on for life. During photosynthesis, forest trees release huge amounts of the oxygen we need for respiration, and they absorb a large amount of carbon dioxide, which would otherwise pollute the atmosphere.

People can help to save forests by buying wood products from well-managed plantations, where new trees are planted for every one that is cut down. Recycling paper can also help. Millions of trees are cut down every year to make paper, but this is an easy product to recycle.

EVIDENCE FOCUS

MAKING RECYCLED PAPER
The reason paper can be recycled is that cellulose fibres are insoluble – they do not dissolve – in water. To make recycled paper, break waste newspaper into small pieces and soak the pieces in a bowl of water. A mushy pulp forms as chemicals in the paper dissolve in water. Spread the pulp out on a flat sieve and leave to drip dry. The recycled paper you make this way is weak. Recycled paper is made stronger by adding chemicals to the pulp, which glue the cellulose fibres together.

▼ Amazonian forests take decades or even centuries to grow, but they can be damaged in a matter of weeks and floated away down the river.

OCEAN RESOURCES

Ocean waters contain important food resources.
And, even though we cannot drink sea water directly,
we can turn it into a freshwater resource.

FISH AND SHELLFISH

Fish and shellfish from the oceans are a major food resource for people around the world. Seafood is low in fat, but high in protein and vitamins, such as A, D, E and B_{12}. The fishing industry provides people with work as well as food, with up to 150 million people worldwide catching, processing and selling seafood.

▶ The huge fishing ships of today use satellite tracking to find fish, and immense nets with small mesh to catch them.

FACT FOCUS

OCEAN PHOTOSYNTHESIZERS

Ocean food chains, which end with fish and fish-eating animals, such as people, begin with tiny floating algae called phytoplankton. About 90 per cent of photosynthesis on our planet happens in the oceans – some scientists claim this produces half the oxygen in the atmosphere. More familiar algae called seaweeds are a widely eaten ocean food resource in countries such as Japan. Algae are also used as thickeners in some products such as toothpaste, for example.

As the population grows, more fish will be needed to help feed the world. Although some fish is farmed, most is caught from wild ocean stocks. Fish should be a renewable resource, but many kinds – such as cod – are being depleted (reduced in numbers) faster than they have a chance to reproduce and replenish. One reason for ocean overfishing is the production of fishmeal to feed to farmed fish, such as salmon. Many countries are now setting limits on how much fish can be caught, in the hope that stocks will recover.

SALT AND WATER

Salt is an essential nutrient and most is obtained from evaporating sea water. Sea water is collected in huge, shallow outdoor lagoons, where the sun gradually evaporates the water, leaving a layer of sea salt.

In parts of the world where fresh water is limited – for example, desert regions such as Saudi Arabia – some people make fresh water from sea water. At a desalination plant, sea water is pushed through a series of very fine, electrically charged membranes that remove the salt, leaving fresh water. At present, this process is expensive, because it uses vast amounts of electricity and produces large amounts of salty brine waste that are hard to dispose of.

OCEAN POLLUTION

The oceans are being damaged by pollution. Large oil spills get lots of coverage in the media, but most oil pollution in the sea comes from industrial waste or used motor oil that people pour down their drains. Much global ocean pollution is sewage and household waste that is dumped directly into the water without being cleaned.

Pollution affects the ocean habitat, harming animals and ecosystems such as coral reefs, and also coastal habitats such as beaches. Coastal areas are an important resource for tourist industries across the world, but no one wants to sit on a dirty beach or swim in a sewage-soiled sea.

▲ Many places could build desalination plants like this one in Dubai to create fresh water from sea water. Some people argue that we should be finding ways to conserve and use less water instead.

▼ More than 270 million litres of oil pollution enter the oceans every year and a lot washes up onto beaches.

FOSSIL FUELS

Fuels are resources that we burn to release energy in the form of light, heat or movement. The fuels that people use most are non-renewable fossil fuels: coal, oil and gas.

FORMATION AND EXTRACTION

Coal started out as dead plants in ancient swamps. Oil and gas started out as tiny marine animals. These remains were buried in sediment underwater. Over time, the movement and accumulation of sediments at the Earth's surface meant that these remains became buried deep under thick layers of rock. Intense pressure and heat converted them into fossil fuels.

People first found fossil fuels on the land surface, when natural gas or crude oil seeped from swamps, for example, or coal washed onto beaches. Over time, people began to dig down to get what they needed, as the surface fuel had been used up. Coal was probably first dug in Stone Age times and the first natural gas well was dug in China in 211 BC. Today, modern technology is used to extract oil and gas from inaccessible places, such as deep beneath the ocean floor.

▼ This is an open-cast coal mine. The 2,000-tonne excavator drags a giant bucket through the ground to dig up coal.

USING COAL AND GAS

People burn some coal and gas to heat water and warm their buildings directly. But most is used to make electricity to operate our factories, lights, computers and other electrical equipment. In power stations, coal and gas are burnt to heat water. The boiling water produces steam and the steam spins immense turbines containing generators. Generators use spinning magnets to convert the 'kinetic energy' of movement into electrical energy.

CRUDE OIL

Crude oil pumped from the ground is a sticky, black mixture of different compounds. In a process called fractional distillation, the crude oil is heated gradually to separate the compounds. Some, such as diesel, petrol, and liquid petroleum gas, are then used as fuels in vehicles. Kerosene is used in boilers to heat buildings, and bitumen is used to make tarmac.

ACID RAIN

Burning fossil fuels releases polluting greenhouse gases, and sulphur and nitrogen oxides. These combine with water vapour in the atmosphere to create acids that fall to

▲ The wide cooling tower at this power station is releasing steam into the atmosphere but the tall chimneys are releasing polluting greenhouse gases.

Earth as acid rain. Acid rain damages leaves on plants, poisons lakes and wears away stone buildings. In 1997, China lost crops and forest worth US$5,000 million because of acid rain.

FACT FOCUS

WHY GAS SMELLS

Natural gas is burnt to produce one fifth of world energy. Natural gas is actually a mixture of gases including methane, ethane, propane and butane. As natural gas is colourless and odourless, a chemical called mercaptan, which smells rather like rotten eggs, is added to it so that people can detect gas leaks. Of all fossil fuels, natural gas burns cleanest, releasing fewer polluting gases than the others.

POLYMERS

Crude oil is not just a resource for fuel. Some parts of crude oil are used as raw materials to make polymers, such as plastic.

▼ Plastic can be used to make artificial joints, like the hip joint shown in the X-ray images below, because it is strong yet light, and can be accurately shaped and stuck to bone.

WHAT ARE POLYMERS?

A polymer is a compound substance made up of chains of molecules. There are some natural polymers, such as the sap from rubber trees

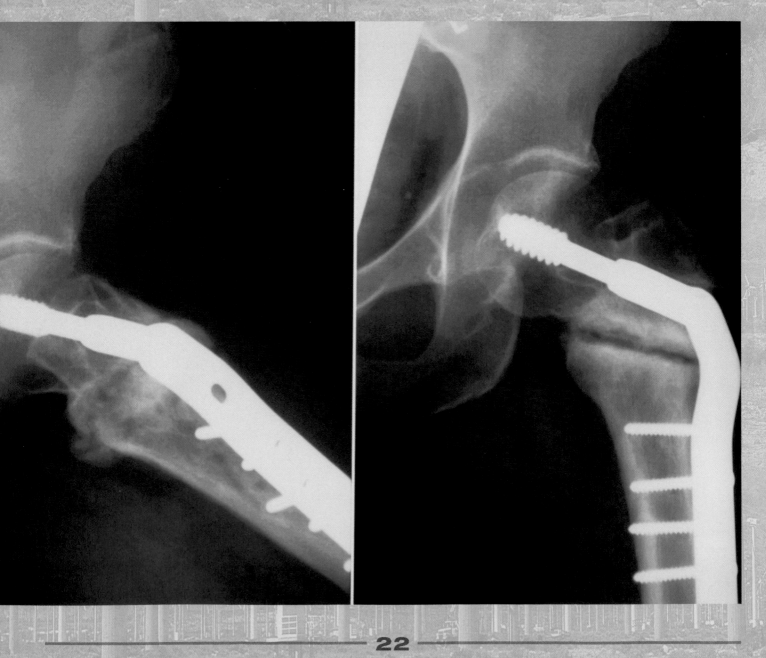

that is used to make tyres. Most polymers are artificial. They are made from crude oil. Different kinds of artificial polymers can be made to have different properties. Some are tough solids, such as the nylon fibres used to make bullet-proof armour. Others, such as acrylic paint, are liquid.

USES OF PLASTICS

Plastics – the most familiar type of polymer – are very useful, because they are waterproof, can be transparent, or any colour or texture, and can be moulded using heat into most shapes. There are seven main types, with different uses. For example, PVC is flexible and used to make plastic bags, garden furniture and water pipes. Tougher PETE is used to make fizzy drink and oil bottles, and light, soft polystyrene is moulded into packing materials to protect goods from knocks.

Plastics can also be mixed with other materials to give different properties. For example, plastic reinforced with fine strands of carbon is used for objects that need to be flexible and withstand enormous stresses, such as helicopter blades or tennis rackets.

STICKING AROUND

Another quality that makes plastic useful is that it does not rot or biodegrade. This is also what makes plastic a problem. Plastic bags can take up to 500 years to decay in landfill sites. Plastic dumped in the oceans floats around, accumulating piles of unsightly waste on coastlines. It is also a hazard to marine animals, as they can eat or become tangled in plastic items.

Many types of plastics can be recycled to make different plastic products. But most countries find it quicker, and cheaper, to burn plastic in waste incinerators. This releases polluting gases, such as dioxins, into the atmosphere. In Japan, where over 70 per cent of waste is burnt, people who live near incinerators have more cancers as a result of breathing in dioxins.

◄ Modern plastic tennis racket frames are reinforced with carbon to remain stable when they hit the ball at high speeds.

CONSTRUCTION MINERALS

Minerals are solid, inorganic components of the rocks that make up our planet. Minerals have many uses. People use some mineral resources to construct homes and buildings, and many other useful things.

ROCKS AND MINERALS

Most rocks are a combination of several different minerals. For example, granite is made up of the minerals quartz, mica and feldspar. Some limestone is made mainly from the mineral calcite, but the majority of limestone is formed from the fossilized skeletons of tiny marine organisms.

Different rock resources are found in different places. Sand and gravel are usually dredged from under the sea, whereas clay often comes from riverbanks. Many rocks are dug from the Earth's surface in quarries and mines, using heavy mechanical machinery and explosives. These activities can leave giant holes in the ground, or piles of waste rock, which have been dug up to get at other rocks. Whole habitats are often ruined as a result.

▲ Construction workers set off several buried explosions at once to break off large pieces of rock from a quarry wall.

BUILDING BLOCKS

In the past, people often used chunks of solid stone to build with. Today, it is too expensive to use extensively, but some stone is still used in buildings, such as slate for roofing tiles. Now it is more common to build with bricks, which are moulded and baked blocks of clay. Bricks or stone blocks are held together using cement. Cement is a powder made by heating and grinding limestone rock with clay and the mineral gypsum. When cement is mixed with water, a chemical reaction sets it hard. Cement is mixed with sand, gravel or crushed rock to make concrete. As these bulk materials are

▶ Marble is often cut and polished for decorative surfaces in buildings. The Taj Mahal in India is built completely of white marble inlaid with beautiful patterns.

heavy to transport, concrete is usually made with whatever is available locally.

Most buildings are now made using concrete, sometimes reinforced with metal bars. It is cheap to process and can be poured into moulds to set into whatever shape is needed.

Glass

Glass is a material made by melting together sand (containing the mineral silicon), ground limestone and soda ash (from the mineral trona), in a hot furnace. Before it hardens, molten glass can be rolled into sheets for use as window panes, roofs and doors.

The ability of glass to transmit and reflect light has been used for centuries to make lenses and mirrors in optical equipment. Today, thin strands of glass are bundled together in fibre-optic cables to transmit digital signals as light pulses between computers around the world.

▼ The glass in this building is strengthened with tough, clear plastic film to make it strong and shatterproof.

FACT FOCUS

IS GLASS SOLID?

Glass is rather different to most solids. All solids have an ordered structure. There is regular spacing between the molecules that make them up. In glass, however, the molecules are in a disordered arrangement with different spaces between them. Solids usually melt to become liquids at a particular temperature. However, glass melts over a range of temperatures. Because it is not quite solid and not quite liquid, glass is described as an amorphous substance.

METALS

Metals are important resources. Most, including iron, aluminium and copper, are found as metallic minerals in rocks called ores. A few metals, such as gold, are found naturally in the Earth.

Coke + iron ore + limestone

IRON AND STEEL

Iron is extracted from iron ores, such as haematite and magnetite. These ores contain different amounts of iron oxide, mixed in with other minerals, including carbon. The oxide is converted to iron by heating with coke fuel in special furnaces. Most of the other minerals form waste slag, which is often used in road building.

Iron containing a lot of carbon is hard, but brittle. Most iron is processed into steel by removing excess carbon. Steel can be worked more easily than iron – for example, rolled when hot and soft into bars, plates and sheets. Other metallic minerals are added to steel, making alloys with different properties. For example, stainless steel contains chromium to make it strong, shiny and rust-resistant.

EXTRACTION OF IRON IN BLAST FURNACE

▶ In a blast furnace, hot air is blown through a mixture of ore, limestone and coke fuel. The limestone removes most impurities in the ore.

Hot waste gases (used to heat air)

Hot air (to burn coke fuel)

Molten iron flows out of the furnace for use

Slag waste floats off

ALUMINIUM

Aluminium is a soft metal used, for example, to make aircraft and car bodies, or household appliances such as fridges. It is usually extracted from bauxite ore, a type of clay mostly found in tropical regions.

Bauxite is crushed, washed and treated with chemicals. This produces a liquid that contains aluminium. Powerful electric currents are passed through the liquid to extract the aluminium.

GOLD AND COPPER

All gold, and some copper, occurs in the Earth as metal, often trapped in rock and sometimes found in river gravel. Gold is a soft metal used in electronics and in jewellery. It is so valuable that even rocks containing as little as 10 grams of gold per tonne of rock are worth mining.

Some rock containing gold also contains copper minerals, such as copper sulphide. Copper is extracted from this ore using heat and electricity. Pure copper is a very good conductor of heat and electricity. It is widely used in heating pipes, electrical wires and in electronic equipment, such as computers.

▲ Parts of vehicles made out of strong, stress-resisting steel range from a ship hull or car chassis to an aircraft turbine.

▼ Gold does not corrode when exposed to air and most gold used in jewellery contains some copper to make it harder.

FACT FOCUS

BLACK SMOKERS

We get some mineral ores from deep beneath the ocean. Water as hot as 380°C rushes out of vents (holes) on the ocean floor, having been heated by contact with hot volcanic rocks. This water contains ore minerals, such as copper, zinc and nickel. These minerals are deposited in chimney-like structures on the surrounding ocean floor, from where they can be harvested. The dark, mineral-rich water bursting from the springs gives them the name 'black smokers'.

CRYSTALS

Crystals are mineral resources that are made up of atoms arranged in regular patterns. The finest natural crystals are often made into expensive gemstones. Many crystals have important industrial and technological uses because of their particular properties.

GEMSTONES

Perfect, large, single crystals of any mineral are unusual, but some are very valuable because they are prized for their colour, clarity and beauty. Colour is determined by traces of

◀ ▼ A ruby dug straight from the ground (left) can be cut into shapes and polished to make sparkling jewellery (below).

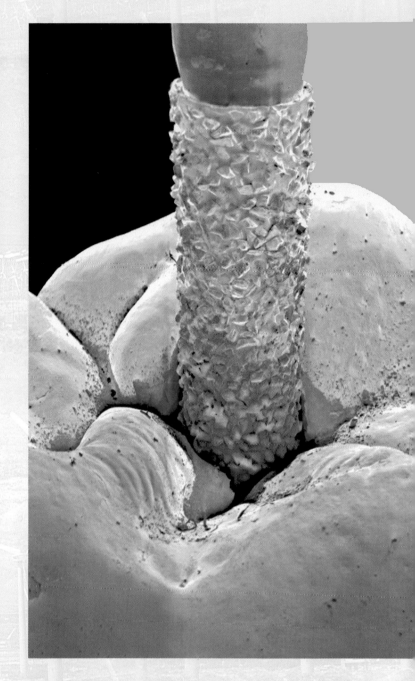

▲ Synthetic diamonds are often glued onto dental drills (as shown magnified here) to make tiny holes in teeth or onto sawblades used to cut hard stone, concrete or glass.

mineral impurities in crystals. For example, a corundum crystal is colourless when pure, but red with a trace of chromium, becoming a ruby, or blue with iron or titanium, becoming a sapphire. Gemstone colours can be made to shine by cutting crystals along certain surfaces and polishing them.

USEFUL CRYSTALS

People make crystals for use in industry and in high-tech applications, from raw materials, such as quartzite and sand, because they are cheaper and much more common than natural crystals. One useful property of crystals is the regular arrangement of the atoms within them, because this controls their response to electricity and light. For example, a quartz crystal cut in a particular way will vibrate 100,000 times per second when an electric current is passed through it. This quartz movement is used to control the time displays on electronic watches and clocks.

Silicon crystals can be used as semiconductors. Semiconductors conduct electricity well or less well depending on, for example, how hot it is or how they are chemically treated. Wafers of silicon are used to make tiny electronic circuits in computers, mobile phones, digital cameras and other devices.

ATOMS AND HARDNESS

The strength of bonds between atoms in a crystal determines its hardness. Diamond is so hard it is useful for cutting other hard materials. Small synthetic (artificial) diamonds are made by squeezing graphite, which is also made of carbon atoms, at high temperature. This mimics the process in which diamonds form naturally underground.

HYDROPOWER

Hydropower is the power of moving water. Moving water, which has kinetic energy, is a resource that can be used to make electricity. The different kinds of hydropower are renewable resources because water is constantly replenished through the water cycle.

HYDROELECTRICITY

Hydroelectric power stations currently provide more than 20 per cent of the world's electricity needs. Most large hydropower stations use a dam built across a river to collect water in a reservoir. Gravity forces the water through pipes to turn a turbine that drives an electricity generator. The water then returns to the river. Some smaller hydroelectric power stations use the force of river water flowing downhill without needing a dam.

▲ This is the Dalles Dam, a hydropower dam on the Columbia River in the USA. It is one of the largest dams in the world.

There are around 45,000 dams across the world and more are being built, but many people see large dams as a problem. Building dams has displaced millions of people and drowned wildlife and habitats. Dams can dry up wetlands usually fed by rivers and cause flooding on normally dry land.

TIDAL ENERGY

In a tidal power scheme a large dam, called a barrage, is built across a river estuary. When the tide goes in and out, the water flows through tunnels in the dam. The movement of the tides is used to turn a turbine, or can be used to push air through a pipe, which then turns a turbine.

Tidal barrages are expensive to build and can disturb the natural movement of tides. This affects river wildlife, such as estuary birds, that feed on small animals in the mud.

WAVE POWER

As wind blows across the surface of the sea it causes waves. Waves are a powerful source of energy. At present, there are few wave power stations because it is difficult to harness this energy in large amounts.

At a wave power station, waves wash in and out of a large chamber of air and force the air in and out of a hole in the top of the chamber.

As the air moves it turns a turbine set inside the hole, which operates a generator.

▼ This is the Limpet Wave Power Station in Scotland, UK. As waves break over it, its generator produces enough electricity for 300 homes.

SOLAR AND GEOTHERMAL POWER

Solar and geothermal power are renewable sources of energy. Solar power systems harness the light and heat energy from the Sun high above Earth. Geothermal power stations convert heat found deep within the planet into a source of energy.

SOLAR PANELS

To produce electricity, solar panels trap the energy from sunlight. The panels are usually sited high on a roof to catch light. The panels are made up of lots of solar cells wired together. Each solar cell consists of two thin layers of silicon set between glass or plastic. When sunlight shines on the upper layer of silicon it creates a tiny electrical current that passes to the lower silicon layer. Electricity from a solar panel is then passed into a building's electricity system. Solar cells don't need bright sunlight to work, but the sunnier it is, the more power each cell makes.

Solar collectors are glass boxes that trap heat energy from the Sun and use it to warm up water as it runs through narrow pipes. This heated water can be passed into taps for washing or cleaning, or into radiator pipes to work central heating systems.

▼ The solar collectors in this picture use the Sun's energy to heat water for a school.

SOLAR POWER

Electricity sourced from solar panels is the biggest source of renewable energy available to us today. It is also a 'clean' form of electricity, because it does not produce polluting gases. The disadvantages of solar power at present are that it is expensive to set up, harness and store on a large scale.

▲ HELIOS is a light, remote-controlled NASA aeroplane with a wingspan of 75 metres and it is powered by solar cells. It flies very high, very slowly and, in future, it could replace expensive communication satellites.

GEOTHERMAL POWER

Deep in the centre of the Earth, temperatures reach 6,000°C, hot enough to melt rock. Even a few kilometres below the surface, it can be 250°C. In some places on Earth, molten rock can be found quite close to the surface.

To harness this geothermal energy, people drill holes, called injection wells, down to a layer of hot rock. Cold water is pumped down to the hot rock, where it heats up. The hot water comes back up another channel under pressure. At the surface, steam from the hot water spins turbines that drive electric generators, or it is passed through pipes to heat water to warm houses. Unused steam is not wasted. It is condensed by evaporation in a cooling tower and pumped back down an injection well to start the process again.

▶ Geothermal power plants store and pipe hot water into generators to convert underground heat energy into electricity.

GEOTHERMAL POWER PLANT

Power lines

Generator

Turbine

Cooling towers

Hot water storage tanks

Production well   Injection well

WIND POWER

Wind power has been used for centuries. Long ago, windmills used the power of moving air to turn wheels to grind corn. Today, we use wind to rotate giant turbines to generate electricity.

HOW WIND GETS ITS ENERGY

Wind is moving air. Energy from the Sun is converted into the kinetic energy of wind. Heat energy from the Sun warms the Earth and the air around the planet unevenly. Areas of warm air rise up in the atmosphere because warm air is lighter and less dense than cold air. Cooler air sinks to fill the gaps from which the warm air has risen. Weather forecasters describe this as air moving from areas of high pressure to areas of low pressure. The greater the difference between the high pressure and low pressure in a particular part of the atmosphere, the greater the speed of the winds there.

USING WIND ENERGY

To capture energy from the wind, we build wind turbines – tall towers with large three- or four-bladed propellers on top. When wind hits the angled, flat surfaces of the blades, it makes them rotate,

◀ When this windmill was in operation, the wooden sails would have been covered with tight canvas, to catch the wind and operate a millstone inside the tower.

turning a generator that produces electricity. The turbines can be twisted to face the wind directly. To produce large amounts of energy a lot of wind turbines are needed. Where many turbines are built together it is called a wind farm.

WHERE TO BUILD WIND FARMS

An average wind speed of about 25 kilometres per hour is needed to generate worthwhile amounts of electricity. Places where wind speeds are usually strong are coastal regions, sometimes out at sea, open plains and at the tops of hills or mountains. The trouble is, many people object to building wind farms in rural and coastal areas because of the way they change the landscape. This is because the propellers are very large and the towers need to be very tall, to get the propellers up high into the wind. Also, large rotating propellers on a wind farm can create quite a lot of noise and kill birds that fly into them.

▼ An offshore wind farm in Denmark. Each turbine can produce enough electricity to meet the needs of around 600 homes every year.

FACT FOCUS

A WIND-POWERED FUTURE?

Between 1 to 2 per cent of all the energy that comes to our planet from the Sun is converted into wind energy. At present, we are unable to capture all this energy, but the British Wind Energy Association estimates that this would be enough to satisfy world energy requirements three times over!

BIOMASS ENERGY

Biomass is plant or animal matter that can be used as, or converted into, fuel. This renewable fuel resource currently provides about 15 per cent of the world's energy.

BIOMASS RESOURCES

All biomass resources, from wood to manure, started life as plants growing and storing the Sun's energy through photosynthesis. Some plants, such as quick-growing trees like willows, are grown specifically as biomass resources. Other biomass plants, such as seaweed, are harvested from the wild. Most biomass energy is made from plant or animal waste. Plant waste includes offcuts from timber yards and residue left after processing crops – including plant stalks, pulp from olives pressed for oil, or juice from sugar cane. Animal waste includes manure from cattle and pigs.

▼ These biogas digesters in China are tanks in which gloopy biomass waste, including manure and rotting waste plants, can be converted into methane gas for fuel.

EARLY ETHANOL

When Henry Ford designed his famous Model T car in 1908, he planned it to run on ethanol. Ford expected ethanol made from corn to be a major fuel. However, high corn prices, problems with storing and transporting ethanol, and the growing oil industry in the USA meant that oil was easier and cheaper to use. By the 1940s, ethanol fuel plants had closed and petrol had taken over.

▲ Pig manure is valuable waste biomass. If all US pig farms made manure into fuel, the USA would need to spend £6 billion less on buying oil each year.

In a new process pioneered in Illinois, USA, diesel fuel is made from pig manure. Using heat and pressure, each litre of pig manure can be converted into 125ml of biomass diesel.

BIOMASS PROS AND CONS

Biomass resources are renewable and there is a potentially endless supply. Using biomass waste also makes sense because it is cheap and eliminates the problems associated with waste disposal.

However, there are problems with biomass energy. For example, worldwide, people cut down 2 million hectares of trees per year for fuelwood, which they use for heat and cooking. If they do not plant trees to replace those they have cut down, the resource is used up and can no longer be considered renewable. Also, burning biomass fuel releases greenhouse gases into the atmosphere.

Some biomass is simply burnt, but some is converted into fuel gas. For example, when natural bacteria rot biomass, such as animal waste, they release methane gas. Methane gas can be collected, stored and piped to stoves and electricity generators.

BIOMASS VEHICLE FUELS

Biomass waste such as sugar cane, maize or cassava contains lots of sugar or starch. These compounds can easily be converted to ethanol, a type of alcohol. Pure ethanol was the major car fuel at the start of the twentieth century. Today, it is usually blended with petrol.

HOW LONG WILL RESOURCES LAST?

We know that non-renewable resources will run out, but how quickly? And what can be done about the renewable resources that are being reduced or damaged by overuse, waste or pollution?

RESOURCE LIFESPAN

At present rates of use, many of the non-renewable resources that we rely on, including fossil fuels and minerals, will run out within the next 100 years. For example, gas may last 60 years, oil about 40 years and gold about 30 years. Supplies of coal might last over 500 years, but as burning coal produces polluting gases that contribute to global warming and air pollution, many people argue we should limit coal use now anyway. In future, it is likely that these energy sources will be replaced by renewable power schemes, such as solar and wind.

However, so-called renewable resources may be under threat, too. Some, such as forests and fish, are being used up faster than they can be replaced. And, in the case of many other resources, such as air and water, the amount available to us is being reduced because of pollution.

POLLUTION PROBLEMS

Around the world, scientists and governments are working on ways to solve pollution problems. For example, the biggest sources of atmospheric pollution are electricity power

◀ In the future, river pollution like this might be reduced by stricter laws and heavier fines for companies and individuals that do not dispose of their waste responsibly.

▼ In some countries of the world, poor families often risk injury and illness by sifting through other people's waste to find things they can sell.

plants and vehicles. Current global solutions include laws requiring vehicles to be fitted with catalytic converters, which reduce carbon emissions. In future, some people predict industries may be charged for any environmental damage they cause to shared resources. For example, air travel is the most polluting form of transport, producing vast quantities of greenhouse gases. Some people say that airlines should pay for the carbon dioxide their planes release into the atmosphere.

OVERUSE AND WASTE

The other major threat to world resources is that people are using them up too rapidly. In the world today, a small proportion of people use far more resources than they need, while many other people do not have enough. Not only does this overconsumption use up certain resources, the waste it produces damages others. Most household waste piles up in landfill sites, rotting down and seeping methane and poisonous liquids into soil and polluting underground water sources. As landfill sites fill up, waste is burnt in incinerators, releasing polluted gases into the air.

SUSTAINABLE RESOURCE USE

Sustainable resource use means using resources more carefully, so they last into the future. To use resources sustainably involves the three Rs: reducing, reusing and recycling.

REDUCING RESOURCE USE

It is easy to reduce the number of resources we use. Start off by buying fewer new clothes, shoes, games and other items. Hire CDs and DVDs, instead of buying new. Carry your shopping in reusable bags rather than the new plastic bags that shops give out. You can use consumer power to help to protect renewable resources. For example, buy wood that comes from managed plantations where new trees are planted to replace those that are cut down, and refuse to eat types of seafood that are being over-fished.

Save fossil fuels by cycling, walking or using the bus instead of the car. Reduce electricity use by switching off lights and machines completely – leaving them on standby still uses 85 per cent as much power as when they are being used. We can also buy low-energy light bulbs and machines with high-energy ratings, which use less electricity to run.

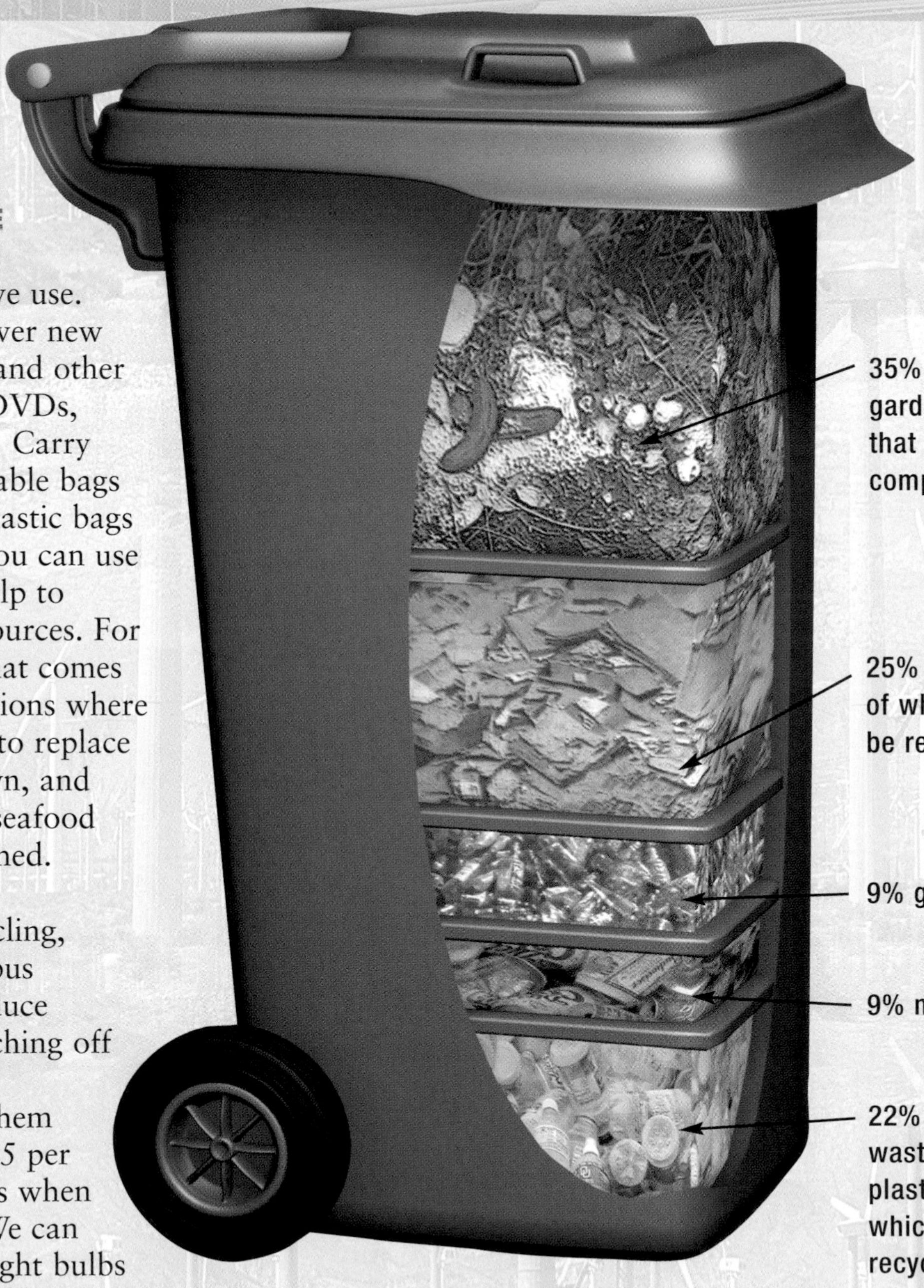

35% kitchen and garden waste that could be composted

25% paper, some of which could be reused

9% glass

9% metals

22% other waste, including plastic, most of which cannot be recycled easily

HOUSEHOLD WASTE

▲ This diagram shows the percentages of different kinds of waste filling an average bin. Look how much could be recycled rather than dumped in landfill sites.

REUSING RESOURCES

Reusing resources means reusing things rather than throwing them away. Repair items instead of replacing them. For example, mend your old bike and give or sell it to someone else to ride when you grow out of it. Clothing and other items can be donated to charity stores to be sold or sent to people who need it. People also find innovative ways of reusing old items. For example, a pile of used tyres makes a good compost bin, or filled with soil it can be used to grow potatoes. Clean out plastic containers and use them for storage or packed lunches, instead of buying new ones.

RECYCLING RESOURCES

Recycling is when things we throw away are converted into something else. Not only does recycling save raw materials, such as trees, oil or minerals, but most recycled products usually

▼ The walls of this Namibian woman's kitchen are made from recycled food and drink cans.

take less energy to make, and therefore create less pollution. For example, used plastic bottles can be turned into fleece jackets, pencils or cups. Aluminium tins and glass bottles can be turned into new cans and bottles.

You can encourage recycling by collecting items to be recycled and choosing to buy recycled products, such as paper, whenever you get the choice.

FACT FOCUS

ALUMINIUM ALLOWANCES
It takes 20 times more energy to make a new aluminium can than a recycled one. It takes 5 tonnes of bauxite ore to make 1 tonne of new aluminium, but none to make recycled tins. Aluminium also has the advantage that it does not degrade or lose quality when used again, so it can be recycled almost indefinitely.

TIMELINE

Here are some of the main discoveries and milestones in the history of people's use of the Earth's resources.

1500 BC Hot springs are used by Romans, Japanese, Chinese and others for bathing, cooking and heating.

200 BC Coal mining starts in China.

AD 100 Ancient Greek engineer Hero of Alexandria experiments with solar-powered pumps and Greeks invent first waterwheel.

1180 Efficient windmills with horizontal sails come into use.

1556 Agricola writes *De Re Metallica*, a book about mining and smelting a variety of metals (extracting metal from ore by melting), plus their effects on habitats, such as woodlands, and the health of mining workers.

1666 Japan's leaders warn against dangers of erosion, stream siltation (filling in of streams and other water channels with soil particles) and flooding caused by deforestation, and urge people to plant tree seedlings.

1690 The recycled paper-making process is introduced in Philadelphia, USA, where a mill makes paper from recycled cotton and linen rag fibre.

1765 Steam engine is perfected by James Watt in the UK.

1799 Alessandro Volta creates the first electric battery called the Voltaic pile, the first source of a steady electric current.

1831 In the UK, Michael Faraday discovers that electricity can be induced by changes in an electromagnetic field.

1852 The Geysers geothermal area in the USA is developed into a spa called The Geysers Resort Hotel.

1852 In the USA, anger over the felling of a giant sequoia tree that was about 2,500 years old leads to calls for the conservation of wild areas. The region around where the tree once stood eventually became Yellowstone National Park.

1854 Daniel Halladay designs the first commercially successful mechanical windmill to pump water in the American Midwest. Over the next 100 years more than 6 million windmills are built to pump water for farm homes and livestock.

1861 French scientist Augustin Mouchot patents his invention of a solar engine.

1865 Natural gas first found near Stockton, California, USA.

1865 English economist W. Stanley Jevons calls attention to the fact that Britain's coal supplies would run out one day.

1871 The US Fish Commission is formed to investigate the decline of coastal fisheries.

1881 A Norwegian geologist blames the grey snow in various parts of the country on long-range air pollution caused by soot and smoke from British industries.

1882 World's first hydroelectric power plant starts operation on the Fox River in Appleton, Wisconsin, USA.

1885 In Germany, Karl Benz builds a three-wheel automobile powered by a gasoline engine and Gottlieb Daimler builds the world's first motorbike.

1908 Swedish chemist Svante Arrhenius argues that what we now call the greenhouse effect from coal and petrol use is warming the globe.

1937 The term 'greenhouse effect' is coined by American assistant professor Glen Thomas Trewartha, to describe the action of short-wave solar energy absorbed at the Earth's surface being transformed into heat, while long wave energy is released back into space. The heat is absorbed by water vapour, carbon dioxide and other gases acting like a pane of glass in a greenhouse.

1941 Before the Second World War, the use of solar power is expanding in the USA – in Miami, 80 per cent of new homes are built with solar hot water. However, due to copper rationing during the war, the solar water heating market declines.

1954 The first nuclear-powered electricity station opens in the former Soviet Union.

1954 The solar cell (or photovoltaic (PV) cell), is discovered by Bell Telephone researchers in the USA.

1961 World Wildlife Fund (now World Wide Fund for Nature) is founded.

1967 The world's first and biggest tidal power plant is opened on the estuary of the River Rance, in western France.

1970 In the USA, 20 million people take part in the first Earth Day demonstration, calling for air and water to be cleaned up and for nature conservation. Earth Day was called 'a day to re-examine the ethic of individual progress at mankind's expense'.

1970–1972 The US government passes acts to tackle air, freshwater and ocean pollution, including the Clean Air Act and the Clean Water Act.

1974 Environmental scientists F. Sherwood Rowland and Mario J. Molina describe the way CFCs (or chlorofluorocarbons) break up ozone in the atmosphere.

1977 Kenya's Green Belt Movement begins with the planting of seven small saplings. By 1992, over 7 million saplings have been planted to prevent desertification in the region.

1980 National Academy of Sciences, USA, says leaded petrol is the greatest source of atmospheric lead pollution.

1986 First phase-out of leaded petrol in the USA is completed.

1988 At the World Conference on the Changing Atmosphere in Canada, a resolution calls for global carbon dioxide emissions to be reduced by 20 per cent by 2005. A UN resolution defines climate as a 'common concern of mankind'.

1988 NASA reports that the ozone layer is being eroded much more quickly than previously predicted. Meanwhile, DuPont – the largest CFC producer – announces it is to substitute CFCs with safer chemicals.

1990 A UN report on climate change warns that global temperatures might rise by as much as 2°F (about 1.1°C) in 35 years. The report recommends reducing carbon dioxide emissions worldwide.

1992 World leaders meet in Brazil at the Earth Summit, a United Nations global conference, set up to find ways to halt the destruction of non-renewable natural resources and tackle pollution.

1997 The Kyoto Protocol is an agreement between countries to reduce the amount of greenhouse gases that their countries produce. The treaty could only come into effect when countries accounting for 55 per cent of world greenhouse gas emissions signed up to it. The USA refused to sign, but when Russia signed in 2005 the treaty came into force.

2002 Second Earth Summit takes place in Johannesburg, South Africa, where leaders discuss global issues, such as trade and food, climate, forests and water.

2004 European Union publishes a pollution register naming the worst polluters.

2009 World's largest solar power station to be completed in Portugal.

2015 Greenhouse emissions from less-developed countries are predicted to exceed those from more-developed countries.

2020 Mount Kilimanjaro predicted to have no snow on top any more as a result of global warming.

2025 African tropical forest predicted to be 30 per cent smaller than in 1990.

2040 Japan plans to build an enormous satellite capable of sending electricity back to Earth from space.

2075 World population should stabilize at about 9 billion.

GLOSSARY

Acid rain Rainwater that has been polluted by chemicals in the air, especially industrial waste gases. Acid rain is damaging to plants, animals and stone buildings.

Alloy Mixture of two or more metals. Brass is an alloy: a mixture of copper and zinc.

Atmosphere Layers of gases that surround a planet.

Atom Smallest particle of a chemical element that can take part in a chemical reaction.

Bacteria Microscopic, single-celled organisms, some of which decompose (break down) dead organisms and waste. Some kinds of bacteria can cause disease.

Biodegrade To be broken down or rotted by bacteria or other living organisms.

Cancer Serious disease in which some cells in the body multiply very quickly, sometimes forming a lump called a tumour.

Carbon dioxide Colourless, odourless gas found in the Earth's atmosphere and formed by respiration. Carbon dioxide is one of the greenhouse gases.

Cell Basic unit of all organisms. Cells are usually microscopic.

Cellulose Carbohydrate that forms the main part of a plant's cell walls.

Compound Substance formed from two or more elements.

Condensation The process that turns water vapour (a gas) into liquid water.

Dam Barrier built to hold back and contain water, often in a reservoir, or to prevent flooding.

Desalination Process by which salt is removed from sea water.

Desertification Process by which an area of land becomes a desert.

Ecosystem Community of plants, animals and other organisms and the habitat they live in.

Evaporation Process of turning from liquid into vapour.

Fertiliser Chemical powders, sprays or liquids used to increase crop yields.

Fossil fuel Natural fuel, such as oil, gas, or coal, which formed from the remains of living things trapped between layers of rock millions of years ago.

Generator Machine that uses spinning magnets to convert movement or kinetic energy into electrical energy.

Global warming Rise in temperatures across the world, caused by the greenhouse effect (see below).

Greenhouse effect Gases in the atmosphere work like the glass in a greenhouse and trap warmth from the Sun, keeping Earth warm.

Greenhouse gas Gas in atmosphere that causes greenhouse effect (see above).

Incinerators Giant ovens for burning waste.

Inorganic Not from a living organism. Inorganic usually refers to mineral substances.

Irrigation Supplying water for crops.

Kinetic energy Movement energy.

Mineral Inorganic substance usually obtained by mining.

Molecule Two or more atoms that are joined together in a chemical compound.

Nutrient Describes a chemical that plants and animals need to grow and survive.

Ore Solid material, such as rock, from which metal or other minerals can be extracted.

Ozone Layer of gas in the atmosphere that prevents harmful radiation from sunlight hitting the Earth.

Pesticide Chemical used to kill insects or other crop pests.

Photosynthesis Process by which plants make glucose in their leaves, using water, carbon dioxide from the air, and energy from sunlight.

Pollution When smoke, dust or other substances damage the air, soil or water in a way that can harm people's health or the environment.

Power stations Factories that make electricity. Many burn fossil fuels, such as coal and gas, to make electricity.

Reservoir Artificial lake that is used for storing water.

Resources Earth materials that we can use. Natural resources include water, soil, air, trees and fossil fuels.

Respiration Process by which organisms release energy from their food.

Sanitation Systems for disposing of sewage and sink waste from houses.

Sediment Very tiny pieces of rock or shells, such as sand or mud, formed by weathering.

Turbine Rotary motor or engine, or a rotating wheel or disc that is driven by wind, water, steam or gas and is used to generate electricity.

UV radiation UV stands for 'ultraviolet'. UV rays come to the Earth from the Sun. They are invisible but can cause sunburn and skin cancer.

Water cycle The continuous movement of water through the atmosphere, land and oceans by the processes of evaporation, condensation and precipitation.

Water vapour Gas formed by evaporation of water. Steam from a boiling kettle is a kind of water vapour.

Weathering When rock is damaged or broken down by wind, rain or other kinds of weather. Weathering can change the surface of the Earth.

FURTHER INFORMATION

Books to read

Atlases of the Earth and Its Resources: The Environment (World Almanac Library, 2004)

Earth's Precious Resources: Soil by Ian Graham (Heinemann Library, 2004)

Eyewitness: Crystal & Gem by R. F. Symes & R. R. Harding (Dorling Kindersley, 2004)

Future Energy by Sally Morgan (Franklin Watts, 2004)

Just the Facts: Sustainable Development by Clive Gifford (Heinemann Library, 2003)

Material Matters: Metals by Carol Baldwin (Raintree, 2005)

Science Essentials – Physics: Energy by Gerard Cheshire (Evans, 2006)

Sustainable Futures: Energy by Sally Morgan (Evans, 2006)

Sustainable Futures: Food for Life by John Baines (Evans, 2006)

Websites

The Science Museum, London
www.sciencemuseum.org.uk/exhibitions/energy/site/EIZc_studies.asp
The Energy Info Zone has some fascinating case studies and stories about energy around the globe.

www.sciencemuseum.org.uk/on-line/challenge/index.asp
The Science Museum's Challenge of Materials page gives lots of information about different materials we use, their properties and what resources are used to make them.

EcoEarth.Info
www.ecoearth.info/
A web portal for a multitude of websites about environmental sustainability.

INDEX